SIMPLY SCIENCE

Mammals

by Vicky Franchino

Content Adviser: Terrence E. Young Jr., M.Ed., M.L.S.,
Jefferson Parish (La.) Public Schools

Reading Adviser: Dr. Linda D. Labbo,
Department of Reading Education, College of Education,
The University of Georgia

COMPASS POINT BOOKS

Minneapolis, Minnesota

Compass Point Books
3722 West 50th Street, #115
Minneapolis, MN 55410

Visit Compass Point Books on the Internet at *www.compasspointbooks.com* or e-mail your
request to *custserv@compasspointbooks.com*

Photographs ©:
Walter Hodges/Corbis, cover; Photri-Microstock/Lani, 4; Roger Rageot/David Liebman, 5; Gail Mooney/Corbis, 6; Thomas Kitchin/
Tom Stack & Associates, 7, 11 bottom, 15; David & Tess Young/Tom Stack & Associates, 8 left; Root Resources/Glenn Jahnke,
8 right; Joe McDonald/Tom Stack & Associates, 9, 16; John Shaw/Tom Stack & Associates, 10; Michael Nolan/Tom Stack & Associates,
11 top, 13 top; David Clobes, 12; Index Stock Imagery, 13 bottom; Dominique Braud/Tom Stack & Associates, 14; Photri-Microstock/
Cheri Roffman, 17; Chris Beddall; Papilio/Corbis, 18; Cheryl A. Ertelt, 19, 21; Inga Spence/Tom Stack & Associates, 20; Robert
McCaw, 23; Root Resources/Loren M. Root, 24; Photri-Microstock, 25; Root Resources/Elizabeth Simms, 26; Index Stock Imagery,
27; Unicorn Stock Photos/Ron Jaffe, 28; Steve Chenn/Corbis, 29.

Editors: E. Russell Primm, Emily J. Dolbear, and Melissa Stewart
Photo Researcher: Svetlana Zhurkina
Photo Selector: Dawn Friedman
Design: Bradfordesign, Inc.

Library of Congress Cataloging-in-Publication Data

Franchino, Vicki.
    Mammals / by Vicki Franchino.
      p. cm. — (Simply science)
    Includes bibliographical references (p.   ) and index.
    Summary: Briefly describes the characteristics shared by all mammals and highlights how various
species are different, discussing habitats, methods of moving around, feeding habits, and life cycles.
    ISBN 0-7565-0032-X (hardcover : lib. bdg.)
      1. Mammals—Juvenile literature. [1. Mammals.] I. Title. II. Simply science (Minneapolis, Minn.)
    QL706.2 .F73 2000
    599—dc21   00-008557

Table of Contents

The World of Mammals

Many kinds of animals live in our world. One group of animals is called the **mammals**. Rabbits, rhinos, cats, cows, horses, hedgehogs, bats, beavers, kangaroos, koalas, platypuses—and people—are all mammals.

Some mammals are very small, and others are huge. One of the smallest

Sheep and llamas are mammals.

You can hold this tiny mammal, ▶
a pigmy shrew, in your hand.

mammals in the world is the pygmy shrew. You could hold this little creature in your hand. The largest mammal on Earth is the blue whale. It may be up to 100 feet (30 meters) long and weigh 260,000 pounds (118,000 kilo- grams)!

This blue whale model hangs in a New York City museum.

The white fur of a snowshoe hare hides it in winter.

All Mammals Have Hair

Some kinds of hair are easy to see. For example, you have hair on the top of your head. The polar bear has a thick coat of fur to keep out the cold. And a snowshoe hare's furry, white coat helps it hide from enemies.

But did you know that hedgehogs, rhinos, and walruses have hair too? A hedgehog's sharp quills are a kind of hair. A rhino's tough horns are also made of hair. And a walrus's whiskers are hair too. Even a whale has a few hairs on its face.

A hedgehog's prickly quills are really hair.

A rhino's horn is made of hair.

Mammals Are Warm-Blooded

Lizards, snakes, and frogs are not mammals. They have to warm up in the sun before they can run around and catch food. Scientists say that these are **cold-blooded** animals.

A mammal does not have to warm up in the sun though. A mammal's body temperature is the same all the time. Scientists say that mam- mals are **warm- blooded**.

Lizards lie in the sun to warm up because they are cold-blooded.

Most of the mammals that live in cold places have thick fur to help them stay warm. Seals and whales have **blubber** to protect them from cold weather.

In the summer, mammals must try to stay cool. People sweat to get rid of heat in their bodies. Dogs pant. Hippos and pigs roll around in mud to stay cool.

Polar bears are warm-blooded.

Whales have blubber under their skins to keep them warm in cold waters.

This elephant takes a mud bath to cool off.

A Mammal's Body

Human beings are mammals, too. So your body has many things in common with the body of a dog, a horse, and a mouse.

Put your hand on the back of your neck and slide it down. Can you feel your **backbone**? It is part of your **skeleton**. The bones that make up your skeleton protect your insides and help you move around. All mammals have a backbone and a skeleton.

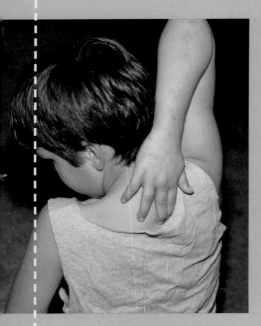

You can feel your backbone on the back of your neck.

You breathe **oxygen** into your lungs. So do all other mammals. Whales and dolphins must lift their heads out of the water to breathe. Fish are not mammals, and they do not have lungs. They use gills to get oxygen out of the water.

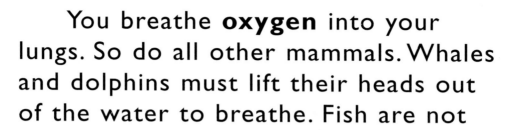

A whale rises out of the water, or breaches, to breathe.

A fish's gills are just behind its eyes.

Sensing the World

Mammals see with their eyes. Rabbits and horses have eyes on the sides of their head so that they can spot enemies all around them. People and monkeys have eyes on the front of their head. This helps them to know how far away things are. Mice and cats can see well at night.

A horse has eyes on the sides of its head.

An orangutan's eyes are on the front is its head.

Most mammals can hear well too. Many mammals use their hearing to help them stay away from enemies. Horses and rhinos can even turn their ears to hear better. Dolphins and bats use sounds to find their way in the dark. They make echoes.

Mammals use **taste buds** on their tongue to taste things. Rats use their taste buds to decide if a food is safe to eat. But some foods that taste bad might actually be good for us!

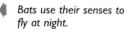

Bats use their senses to fly at night.

Dogs pant to stay cool. ▶

People use touch to decide if something is dangerous. Moles use touch to find their way around in dark underground tunnels.

Mammals smell with their nose. Dogs use smell to find things. Reindeer and seals use smell to find each other. Skunks produce a bad smell to keep their enemies away.

A mole coming out of its tunnel

A skunk raises its tail when it is spraying.

What Do Mammals Eat?

Adult mammals eat many kinds of foods, but all young mammals drink their mother's milk. Mother mammals produce the milk for their babies until they are old enough to find their own food. As mammals grow, they drink less milk and eat more solid food. Giraffes and zebras eat plants. Wolves and lions hunt other animals and eat their meat.

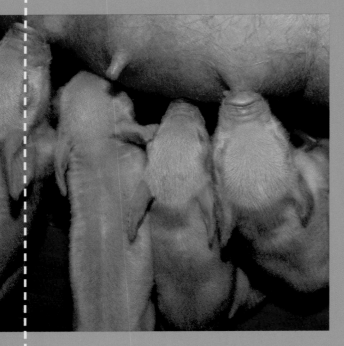

Newborn piglets drink their mother's milk.

A giraffe's long neck lets it reach tree leaves to eat.

Moles, shrews, and aardvarks spend most of their time eating insects.

Many kinds of mammals eat a variety of foods. Bears eat fish, fruit, and leaves. Rats eat nuts, seeds, leaves, and other tasty treats. A raccoon will eat just about anything. What do you like to eat?

A grizzly bear catching a fish ▶

How Are Mammals Born?

Most young mammals grow inside their mother's body until they are ready to be born. Some mother mammals give birth to many babies at the same time.

Most baby mammals have no teeth and no fur when they are born. They cannot see or hear. Their parents take care of them for several days, weeks, or even months. Human parents take care of their children for many years.

A cat can have many kittens at once.

Some mammals are born before they are fully developed. A tiny kangaroo baby crawls into a pouch on its mother's belly. The baby stays inside the warm, safe pouch until it is big enough to live on its own.

The spiny anteater and the duck-billed platypus are very unusual mammals. They hatch from eggs!

A duck-billed platypus is an odd-looking mammal.

Where Do Mammals Live?

Mammals are found all over the world. No matter where they live, mammals have special features that help them to survive.

Some mammals live in places that are very hot. Sloths and tapirs live in tropical rain forests. Other mammals live in cold places. Polar bears and seals live near the North Pole.

◀ *A sea otter spends most of its time in water.*

Seals can live in very cold water. ▶

Some mammals live in places that are very wet. Otters and beavers spend most of their time in the water. Other mammals live in dry places. Camels and kangaroo rats can live in deserts.

People can live anywhere. We have learned how to make clothes and build homes to keep us warm. We also use air conditioners to stay cool. We build boats to stay dry. And we dig deep wells to get all the water we need. People are pretty incredible mammals!

Camels can go without water for a long time in the desert.

People use their brains to make life easier and more comfortable.

Glossary

backbone—the set of bones that run down the center of a mammal's back; the spine

blubber—a thick layer of fat

cold-blooded—an animal whose body temperature changes as its environment changes

mammals—warm-blooded animals that have hair and drink mother's milk when they are young

oxygen—a chemical in the air that we need to breathe

skeleton—all the bones in the body. The skeleton protects an animal's insides and helps it move around.

taste buds—tiny structures on the tongue that make it possible to taste food

warm-blooded—an animal that has the same body temperature no matter how its environment changes

Did You Know?

- You are closely related to chimpanzees, gorillas, and orangutans.
- Mammals move in many different ways. People walk, kangaroos hop, whales swim, and bats fly.

Want to Know More

At the Library

Giesecke, Ernestine. *Mammals*. Des Plaines, Ill.: Heinemann Library, 1999.

Kalman, Bobbie. *What Is a Mammal?* New York: Crabtree, 1998.

Rabe, Tish. *Is a Camel a Mammal?* New York: Random House, 1998.

Sill, Cathryn P. *About Mammals: A Guide for Children.* Atlanta, Ga.: Peachtree, 1997.

On the Web

The Animal Channel

http://www.animalchannel.net/

For information about keeping pets and protecting wild animals

Animal Photo Library

http://www.si.edu/natzoo/photos/phoset.htm

For pictures of animals at the National Zoo in Washington, D.C.

Endangered Animals

http://tqjunior.thinkquest.org/5394/

For information about and drawings of birds, mammals, water creatures, and more

Through the Mail

The National Marine Mammal Laboratory

7600 Sand Point Way NE F/AKC4

Seattle, WA 98115-0070

To find out more about research being done by scientists who study mammals

On the Road

Denver Zoo

2300 Steele Street

Denver, Colorado 80205

303/376-4800

To see a variety of interesting mammals from all over the world

Index

About the Author

Vicky Franchino has wanted to be a writer ever since she was a young girl and spent hours writing copy for fictional catalogs. As a freelance writer, she has worked for such varied groups as educational toy companies, greeting-card companies, and universities. She holds a bachelor's degree from the University of Wisconsin in Madison. Vicky Franchino lives with her husband and their three daughters in Wisconsin.